GREAT BRITISH
ARCHITECTS

Theodore Rowland-Entwistle
and the Diagram Group

Franklin Watts
London New York Sydney Toronto

A young architect consulting with an experienced professional

Acknowledgements
Picture research: IKON
Cover: Wimpey Group Services
BBC Hulton Picture Library: 30
Richard Bryant: 32
C.O.I.: 2
Country Life: 28
East Anglian Times: 35
Mansell Collection: 6, 9, 10, 11, 12, 15, 18, 20, 21, 23,
Museum of London: 9
National Portrait Gallery: 8, 11
RIBA: 25
University of Glasgow: 27

Contents

© Diagram Visual Information Ltd 1986

First published in Great Britain 1986 by
Franklin Watts Ltd
12a Golden Square
London W1

Printed in Singapore

ISBN 0 86313 368 1

When they lived

1756–1763 Seven Years' War in Europe

1588 Spanish Armada

1642–1651 English Civil War

| 1550 | 1600 | 1650 | 1700 | 1750 |

Inigo Jones
1573–1652

Sir Christopher Wren
1632–1723

Nicholas Hawksmoor
1661–1736

Sir John Vanbrugh
1664–1726

Robert Adam
1728–1792

American
aration of Independence

1854–1856
Crimean War

1897   Queen Victoria's
Diamond Jubilee

1961–1973   Vietnam War

5

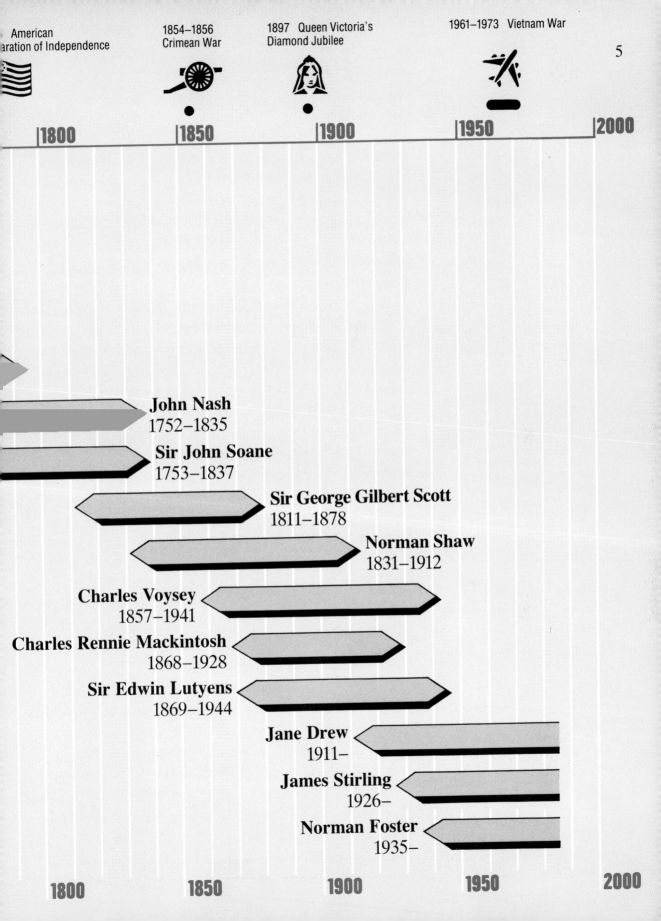

|1800 |1850 |1900 |1950 |2000

John Nash
1752–1835

Sir John Soane
1753–1837

Sir George Gilbert Scott
1811–1878

Norman Shaw
1831–1912

Charles Voysey
1857–1941

Charles Rennie Mackintosh
1868–1928

Sir Edwin Lutyens
1869–1944

Jane Drew
1911–

James Stirling
1926–

Norman Foster
1935–

1800   1850   1900   1950   2000

Inigo Jones

Inigo Jones brought about a revolution in English architecture, based on his study of Italian work. He was the son of a London cloth-worker, and as a youth showed great talent as a painter. Jones made two visits to Italy. The first, in 1601-1603, was paid for by the Earl of Pembroke. The second, in 1613-1614, was in the service of the Earl of Arundel.

Jones made his name as the designer of scenery for musical dramas known as masques, first at the court of Denmark, and later for King James I of England.

In 1615, after his second trip to Italy, Jones was appointed Surveyor of Works to the king, a post he held for 27 years. He quickly gained a reputation for being vain and bossy. His work as Surveyor was the building or rebuilding of royal houses. This he did in the Palladian style, which was a complete contrast to the less formal style that had been common in England.

Jones' first important building was the Queen's House at Greenwich, now the home of the National Maritime Museum. His masterpiece is the Banqueting House at Whitehall, designed to be part of a huge new palace that was never built. His plans for this palace still exist.

In addition to his work for the royal family, Jones built houses for noblemen. He also created London's first squares when he laid out Covent Garden and Lincoln's Inn Fields.

Jones' royal appointment came to an end with the outbreak of the English Civil War in 1642, but he continued to design houses, notably part of Wilton House in Wiltshire for the Earl of Pembroke, brother of his old patron.

Costume designs by Inigo Jones for a masque

The Banqueting House, Whitehall, London

Chimneypiece design in the Single Cube Room at Wilton House, Wiltshire

1573
Born 15th July in London
1601-1603
First visit to Italy
1604-1605
Stage designer at the court of Denmark
1605
Began stage design for the court for James I
1613-1614
Second visit to Italy
1615
Became Surveyor of Works to the king
1616
Began work on the Queen's House, Greenwich
1619-1622
Rebuilt the Banqueting House at Whitehall
1623-1627
Rebuilt the Queen's Chapel at St James' Palace
1630
Laid out Covent Garden and designed its church
1634-1642
Restored old St Paul's Cathedral
1642
Forced to give up his post as Surveyor of Works
1652
Died 21st June in London

Sir Christopher Wren

1632
Born 20th October in East Knoyle, Wiltshire
1649-1653
Studied at Oxford University
1657
Appointed Professor of Astronomy at Gresham College, London
1661-1673
Professor of Astronomy at Oxford University
1663
Designed chapel for Pembroke College, Cambridge
1664
Designed the Sheldonian Theatre, Oxford

Probably the most versatile of British architects was Christopher Wren, who grew up during the turmoil of the English Civil War. Wren studied mathematics and astronomy at Oxford University. He was appointed Professor of Astronomy at Gresham College in London in 1657, and held a similar post at Oxford from 1661 to 1673.

In 1663 his uncle, the Bishop of Ely, persuaded him to design a chapel for Pembroke College, Cambridge. Soon after he was asked to design the Sheldonian Theatre at Oxford. In 1666 he was invited to suggest designs for restoring St Paul's Cathedral in London, which was in such poor condition it was about to collapse.

A week after his plans were accepted the narrow, winding streets of London were ravaged by fire. At once Wren submitted a plan for rebuilding London with wide streets, but for economic reasons it could not be carried out. However, he was asked to supervise the rebuilding of St Paul's and 51 churches to replace the 87 burned. In 1669 he became Surveyor of Works to the king.

Work on St Paul's began in 1675, and was

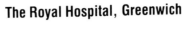

The Royal Hospital, Greenwich

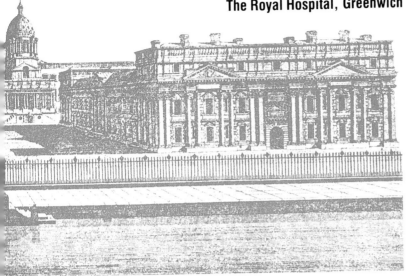

St Paul's Cathedral, London

finished in 1711. While work on rebuilding London was going on, Wren was busy designing other buildings, including the Royal Hospital at Chelsea, and alterations to three royal palaces - Whitehall, Kensington and Hampton Court. His last work was the Royal Hospital at Greenwich.

Wren is buried in St Paul's. Near his tomb is the simple inscription: *Lector, si monumentum requiris, circumspice* (Reader, if you need a monument, look around you).

1666
Great Fire of London
1669-1718
Surveyor of Works to the king
1673
Knighted by Charles II
1675-1711
Designed and rebuilt St Paul's Cathedral
1680-1682
President of the Royal Society
1689
Began work on Kensington and Hampton Court palaces
1723
Died 25th February in London

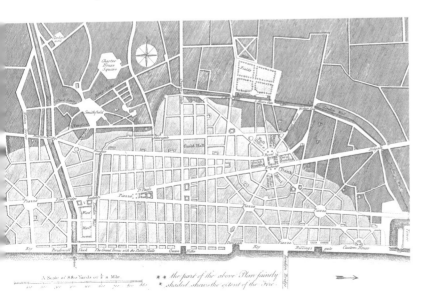

Wren's plan for the new city after the Great Fire of London in 1666

Nicholas Hawksmoor

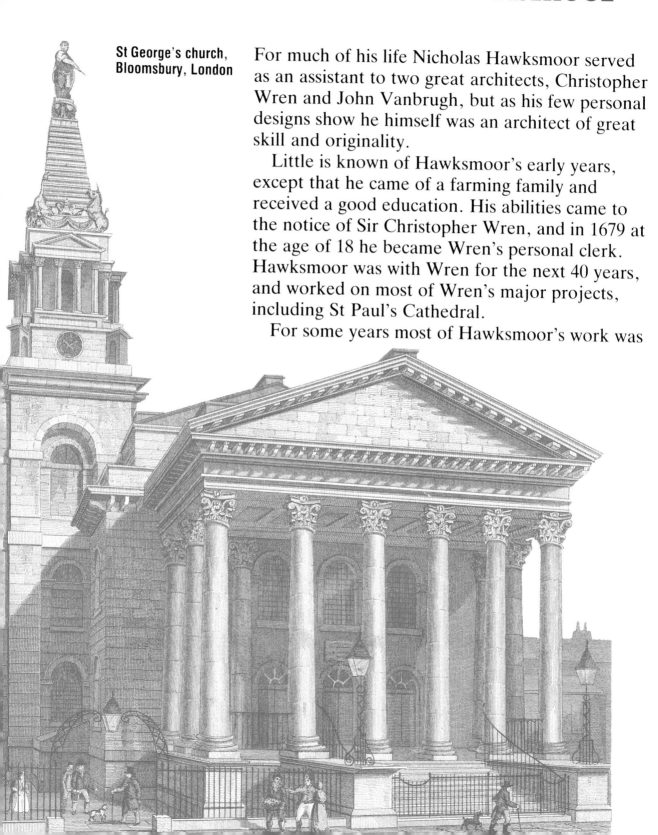

St George's church, Bloomsbury, London

For much of his life Nicholas Hawksmoor served as an assistant to two great architects, Christopher Wren and John Vanbrugh, but as his few personal designs show he himself was an architect of great skill and originality.

Little is known of Hawksmoor's early years, except that he came of a farming family and received a good education. His abilities came to the notice of Sir Christopher Wren, and in 1679 at the age of 18 he became Wren's personal clerk. Hawksmoor was with Wren for the next 40 years, and worked on most of Wren's major projects, including St Paul's Cathedral.

For some years most of Hawksmoor's work was

Three of Hawksmoor's London churches

either as a draughtsman, drawing or copying designs for buildings, or supervising and organising work on Wren's behalf. By the time he was in his 30s, however, Hawksmoor was designing buildings on his own account.

In 1699 Hawksmoor was also working with another architect, John Vanbrugh. It was a very successful partnership, with Hawksmoor at first providing most of the technical skill. One of their outstanding achievements was Blenheim Palace in Oxfordshire for the Duke of Marlborough, and Hawksmoor completed the work after Vanbrugh quarrelled with the Duchess of Marlborough in 1716. Meanwhile he played a large part in the work on Wren's Greenwich Hospital, where he was Clerk of the Works and, for a time, Assistant Surveyor.

Hawksmoor's own designs included the Clarendon Building, home of the Oxford University Press, and he designed or inspired several college buildings in Oxford. He was a surveyor to a commission appointed to build 50 new churches in London, and himself designed six of them. Not long before he died he designed the west towers of Westminster Abbey.

1661
Born, probably in East Drayton, Nottinghamshire
1679
Began working for Sir Christopher Wren
1689
Clerk of the Works at Kensington Palace
1690-1693
Built Broadfield Hall, near Buntingford, Hertfordshire
1698-1736
Clerk of the Works at Greenwich Hospital
1699
Formed working partnership with John Vanbrugh
1709
Designed the Clarendon Building, Oxford
1711
Named as a surveyor to commission for building new churches in London
1715-1718
Clerk of the Works at Palace of Whitehall
1734
Designed west towers of Westminster Abbey
1736
Died 25th March at Millbank, London

Sir John Vanbrugh

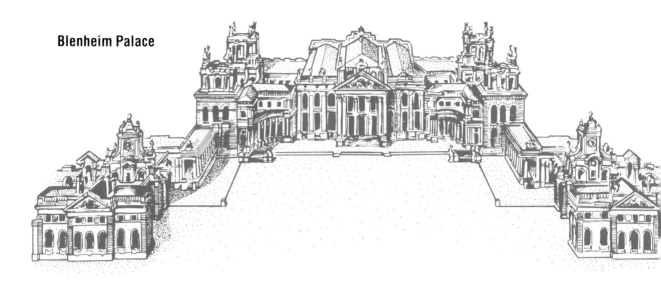

Blenheim Palace

Like his great contemporary Christopher Wren, John Vanbrugh was a man of many talents who became an architect without any training. He was the grandson of a Belgian merchant, and was born in London but brought up in Chester, where his father was a wealthy tradesman.

In 1686 Vanbrugh served for a time as an officer in an English regiment. Four years later he was arrested while visiting France in wartime, and was imprisoned as a spy. During his two years in jail he wrote a comedy, *The Relapse.* When he returned to London he rejoined the army for a further six years. Meanwhile Vanbrugh's plays became popular and his charm and wit made him many friends in high places. Among them was the Earl of Carlisle, who invited him to design a house.

Vanbrugh knew little about architecture, but he was able to form a partnership with Wren's assistant, Nicholas Hawksmoor. Together they created Castle Howard in Yorkshire for Carlisle, who was so pleased that he obtained for Vanbrugh

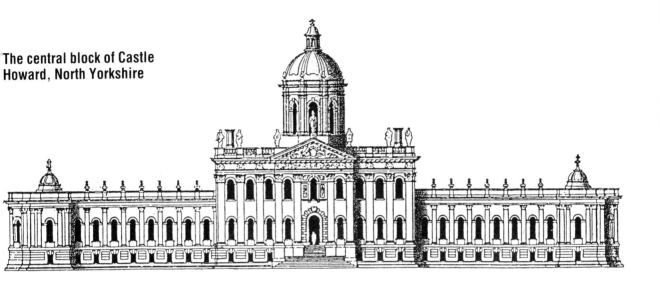

The central block of Castle Howard, North Yorkshire

the post of Comptroller of the Queen's Works, which made him Wren's chief colleague. Soon afterwards Carlisle had him appointed Clarenceux King of Arms, a senior post at the Heralds' College. In 1705 Vanbrugh secured the biggest architectural commission of the time, to build Blenheim Palace at Woodstock in Oxfordshire. This vast building was the gift of the nation to the first Duke of Marlborough, a brilliant general who had won many victories over the French. Again Hawksmoor was Vanbrugh's partner, and he finished the work after Vanbrugh fell out with the Duchess of Marlborough.

The Duchess had Vanbrugh dismissed from his post as Comptroller, but when George I succeeded Queen Anne on the throne Vanbrugh was restored to favour and was knighted.

1664
Baptised 24th January in London
1686
Joined the army
1690-1692
Imprisoned as a spy by the French
1696
First comedy, *The Relapse,* staged at Drury Lane
1699
Began designing Castle Howard with Nicholas Hawksmoor
1702
Appointed Comptroller of the Queen's Works
1704
Appointed as Clarenceux King of Arms
1705
Began work on design of Blenheim Palace
1714
Received a knighthood
1719
Married Henrietta Yarborough, 30 years his junior
1726
Died 26th March in London

Robert Adam

1   2

1728
Born 3rd July in Kirkcaldy, Fife
1746
Began working for his father
1748
Became a partner with his elder brother John
1754-1758
Toured Italy
1758
Set up practice in London
1761
Appointed Architect of the King's Works

Robert Adam was the most brilliant of four Scottish brothers, all architects. The four - John, Robert, James and William - were the sons of Scotland's leading architect, William Adam, who held the official post of Master Mason to the Board of Ordnance. Robert, the second son, was born in 1728, and went to work for his father at the age of 18.

After William's death John succeeded him as Master Mason, and took Robert into partnership. The next six years were prosperous ones for the brothers. By 1754 Robert had saved £5,000, and was able to accept an invitation to accompany the Hon. Charles Hope, brother of the Earl of Dumfries, on a visit to Italy.

Hope introduced Robert into society, but after a few weeks the young architect abandoned high life in favour of serious study. He was accompanied by a new friend, the French architect

3   **4**

and draughtsman Charles-Louis Clarisseau. The two spent almost three years studying and drawing ancient Roman architecture.

When his money ran out Robert returned to Britain and set up in practice in London. Five years later he was joined by his brother James, who had also had a tour with Clarisseau. The brothers created a fresh-looking style of architecture, based partly on the Palladian style and partly on the Italian Renaissance ideas of the 1400s and 1500s.

For much of his time Robert was kept busy with commissions to remodel existing houses. He designed not only rooms, but also all the furniture and fittings for them. In his later years Robert designed a number of important buildings, including the Register House and the University of Edinburgh. He also built a number of sham castles, such as Culzean Castle in Ayrshire.

1 Wall decorations of an interior
2 A London coffee house
3 Design for a carpet
4 A London town house

1763
Joined by his brother James in practice in London
1867
Designed Kenwood House, London
1768-1772
Built the Adelphi, London
1768-1784
MP for Kinross
1772
Designed Register House, Edinburgh
1789
Designed University of Edinburgh buildings
1792
Died 3rd March in London

John Nash

Cumberland Terrace, London

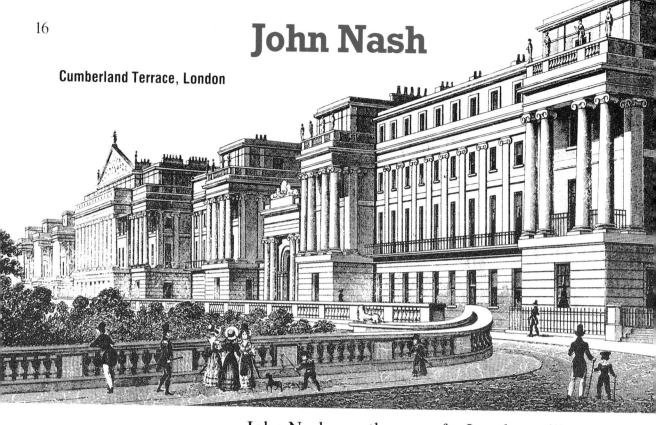

John Nash was the son of a London millwright and engineer. He trained in the office of a fashionable London architect, Robert Taylor. Nash set up in business on his own in 1778 with money left to him by an uncle, but some unsuccessful property deals made him bankrupt, and he retired to Carmarthen.

In Wales Nash made a fresh start, and built a number of country houses. In 1796 he returned to London, where he formed an informal partnership with Humphry Repton, the leading landscape gardener of the day. Nash came to the notice of the Prince of Wales, and was soon rich enough to build a country house for himself, East Cowes Castle on the Isle of Wight.

In 1811 the Prince of Wales became Prince Regent, taking over the powers of his father, George III, who had become insane. By now Nash was the prince's personal architect. For the prince Nash laid out a garden suburb in what had been

The new Regent Street, London

The Royal Pavilion, Brighton

Marylebone Park. The result was Regent's Park, with houses around three sides. To link the park with the prince's home, Carlton House in Pall Mall, Nash built Regent Street, which was completed in 1825. By that time the prince had become King George IV. Most of Regent Street was rebuilt a hundred years later.

Nash's other work in London included Trafalgar Square and the conversion of Buckingham House into Buckingham Palace. The triumphal arch he built as an entrance was moved in 1850, and is now known as Marble Arch. Nash remodelled the Royal Pavilion, Brighton, used as a seaside home by the Prince Regent, in a wild mixture of Indian and classical European styles, using stucco (plaster) on brick to imitate elaborate stonework. Nash owed all his success to George IV's friendship, and when the king died in 1830 Nash's career came to a sudden end.

1752
Born in London
1778
Set up in business as an architect
1783
Became bankrupt and moved to Carmarthen
1796
Returned to London
1798
Married and gained the patronage of the Prince of Wales
1811-1825
Laid out Regent's Park and Regent Street
1815-1823
Remodelled Royal Pavilion, Brighton
1821-1830
Worked on Buckingham Palace
1835
Died 13th May in Cowes, Isle of Wight

Sir John Soane

Section through Sir John Soane's house

1753
Born 10th September in Goring-on-Thames, near Reading
1768
Worked for George Dance
1776
Won the Gold Medal of the Royal Academy
1778-1780
Toured Italy
1784
Married Elizabeth Smith
1788-1833
Architect to the Bank of England
1815-1832
Architect responsible for royal palaces
1831
Received knighthood
1837
Died 20th January in London

John Soane, the son of a builder, got his training in the offices of two London architects, George Dance and Henry Holland. In 1776 he won the Royal Academy's Gold Medal for architecture, and a travelling scholarship which gave him a chance to study in Italy for two years. In Rome he met several wealthy Englishmen who later gave him work.

Soane also met the Bishop of Derry who lured Soane to Ireland with promises of work, but then changed his mind leaving Soane penniless and jobless. Soane returned to London in 1780 and slowly built up a practice with the aid of the rich patrons he had met on his travels.

In 1788 Soane was appointed architect to the Bank of England, which brought him not only a salary but also some useful contacts. Two years

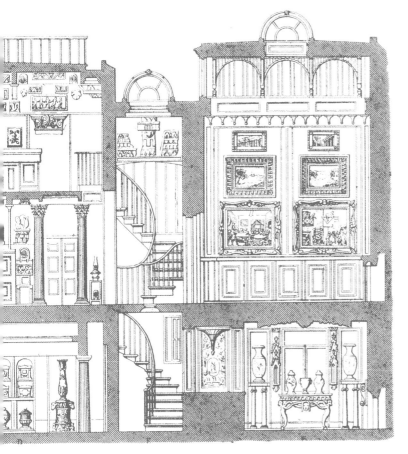

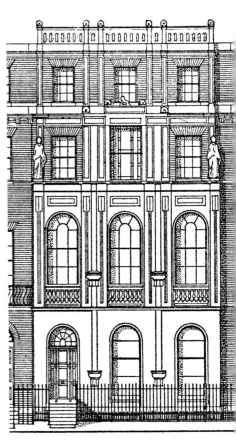

Sir John Soane's design for the front of his house in London

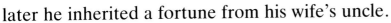

later he inherited a fortune from his wife's uncle.

Over the next 40 years Soane gradually rebuilt the Bank of England as a complex arrangement of halls and courts, surrounded by a wall that was windowless for security reasons, but richly decorated. He also took on further appointments, including that of Professor of Architecture at the Royal Academy, and responsibility for work on the palaces at Hampton Court, Kew, Richmond, Westminster and Whitehall. He accepted few private commissions, except from old friends. In 1831 he was knighted.

His inherited fortune enabled Soane to amass a collection of art and antiques, which furnished the house he built for himself in Lincoln's Inn Fields, London. This house is a now a museum.

Sir George Gilbert Scott

For nearly 40 years George Gilbert Scott was Britain's leading church architect. He worked on hundreds of churches, mostly as a restorer. He has often been criticised for being too ruthless in his restoration work, which led to the founding of the Society for the Protection of Ancient Buildings, but he probably saved much more than he destroyed because so many of the churches he worked on were in very poor condition.

Scott, the son of a country parson, set up in business with a partner, W. B. Moffat, in 1834. Their first commissions were to design and build workhouses. They also built seven churches.

In 1839 Scott became interested in the Gothic architecture of the Middle Ages, and studied it closely. His first venture in this style was the Martyrs' Memorial in Oxford. He followed it by winning a competition to design the new Lutheran Nikolaikirche (Church of St Nicholas) at Hamburg

The hotel and railway station, St Pancras, London

in Germany, which he did in the style of the 1200s. This building made his reputation as a church architect.

Soon afterwards he and Moffat separated. Scott's first important restoration work was on Ely Cathedral, and over the years he went on to restore another 38 cathedrals and minsters. Altogether Scott worked on about 730 buildings.

His new buildings included the Albert Memorial in London (which earned him a knighthood), chapels for Exeter College, Oxford and St John's College, Cambridge, and the vast Gothic St Pancras hotel and railway station in London.

One of Scott's few non-Gothic designs was for the India Office and Foreign Office at Whitehall in London. The Prime Minister, Lord Palmerston, insisted that if Scott did not use the 'classical' style, based on Greek and Roman architecture, he would not get the work.

1811
Born 13th July in Gawcott, Buckinghamshire
1834-1846
In partnership with W. B. Moffat
1840
Built the Martyrs' Memorial in Oxford
1844
Won competition to design Nikolaikirche, Hamburg
1847
Restored Ely Cathedral
1861
Designed new government offices in Whitehall
1862-1872
Built the Albert Memorial
1865
Designed St Pancras hotel and railway station
1878
Died 27th March in London

The Albert Memorial, London

Norman Shaw

1831
Born 7th May in Edinburgh
1845
Moved to London
1849
Articled to architect William Burn
1854-1856
Toured Europe
1859
Assistant to church architect George Edmund Street
1862
Set up in private practice
1873
Designed Lowther Lodge, London
1875
Designed 'Wispers', Midhurst
1876-1880
Helped lay out Bedford Park
1877
Elected a member of the Royal Academy
1886-1890
Built New Scotland Yard
1896
Retired from full-time practice
1912
Died 17th November in London

House building in the later part of the 19th century owes a lot to Richard Norman Shaw, a leader of what has been called the 'Domestic Revival' in British architecture. He once claimed that he was 'a house man and not a church man, and soil pipes are my speciality', though he did build several churches.

Norman Shaw (he did not use his first name) was born in Edinburgh in 1831 of Irish-Scottish parents. His father died when he was two. The family moved to London in 1845, and soon after Shaw began what was in effect a 16-year apprenticeship before he felt ready to branch out on his own.

Shaw set up in practice in 1862, sharing offices for several years with his great friend W. Eden Nesfield. Together they evolved a fresh style for building English country houses, based on the architecture of the 1500s and 1600s.

Shaw proved to be a very versatile architect, and the houses he built varied in design to suit their owners and their location. For example, 'Wispers' at Midhurst in West Sussex imitates the Elizabethan half-timbered style, while Bryanston in Dorset is in a style half Dutch, half Palladian.

The town houses Shaw built are mostly in the Queen Anne style, though Lowther Lodge in Kensington is more like a country house in design. It is now the headquarters of the Royal Geographical Society.

Shaw's only public building was New Scotland Yard, on the Embankment, a mixture of granite and red brick. For many years the headquarters of the Metropolitan Police, it is now used as offices. He also helped to lay out Bedford Park in West London, the first garden suburb.

A private house in Sussex designed by Norman Shaw

Views of New Scotland Yard, London

Charles Voysey

The work of Charles Francis Annesley Voysey comes between the traditionalism of the 19th century and the so-called modernism of the 20th century. Voysey was born at Hessle, near Hull, the son of the Reverend Charles Voysey, a clergyman who was expelled from the Church of England for his unorthodox views on religion. Young Charles was also unorthodox - in his attitude to architecture.

Voysey had little formal education, and later in life he said that he became an architect because it was the only profession he could enter without passing examinations. However, he spent eight years training in the offices of two architects and set up on his own when he was 25.

His first major commission was to build the South Devon Sanatorium at Teignmouth. In his early years he was not merely an architect, but a designer of fabrics, furniture, stained glass and wallpaper. By 1890 he had evolved what became

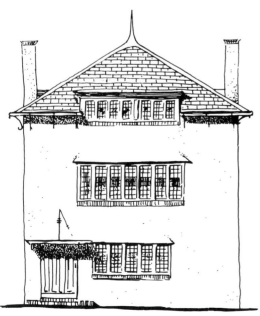

A Voysey sketch design for a house

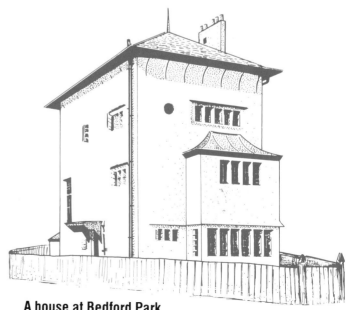

A house at Bedford Park, London

known as the 'Voysey style' of domestic architecture. He used traditional materials. His designs were simple and uncluttered, with no formality about their layout. The houses were designed very much from the inside, rather than by fitting the interior somehow into a handsome shell. Voysey's contemporaries admired his attention to detail. His typical country house had a long, low roof covered with green or grey slates, small leaded windows, and low ceilings.

After the outbreak of World War I in 1914, Voysey's style fell out of favour and he refused to change it to meet the requests of his clients. He did, however, design some of the war memorials which were erected in almost every town and village after the war. Not long before he died he received belated recognition, the Gold Medal, from the Royal Institute of British Architects.

1857
Born 28th May in Hessle
1874-1879
Pupil of architect John Seddon
1880-1882
Assistant to architect George Devey
1882
Set up in practice in London
1885
Married Mary Maria Evans
1890-1914
Built many country and town houses
1929
Elected a Fellow of the Royal Institute of British Architects
1940
Awarded RIBA's Gold Medal
1941
Died 12th February in Winchester

The lounge hall of a country house

Charles Rennie Mackintosh

In the 1880s some artists began to move away from the imitation of the past which had characterised many forms of art for several hundred years. This movement became known as Art Nouveau ('new art'). In architecture one of its greatest pioneers was the Scottish architect Charles Rennie Mackintosh.

The son of a Glasgow policeman, Mackintosh was apprenticed for five years to a local architect, then joined a new firm, Honeyman and Keppie, as a draughtsman. In his spare time he attended evening classes at the Glasgow School of Art. At the school he teamed up with a fellow architect, J. Herbert McNair, and two sisters studying drawing, Margaret and Frances Macdonald. Together 'The Four', as they became known, produced a series of Art Nouveau works in many forms, from fabrics to watercolours. McNair later married Frances, and Mackintosh married Margaret.

Mackintosh gained considerable fame for the

1868
Born 7th January in Glasgow
1884-1889
Apprenticed to architect John Hutchinson
1885-1892
Studied at the Glasgow School of Art
1889-1913
Worked with Honeyman and Keppie
1896
Began work on Glasgow School of Art building
1897-1904
Decorated Miss Cranston's Tearooms in Glasgow
1900
Married Margaret Macdonald; exhibited designs for rooms in Vienna
1915
Set up in business in London
1923-1927
Retired to France to paint
1928
Died 10th December in London

Designs for three studios in Chelsea, London

furniture and interior decoration he designed for a series of tea-rooms in Glasgow, and for some rooms he designed in Vienna.

As assistant to Honeyman and Keppie - he did not become a partner until 1902 - Mackintosh designed a number of buildings, but the only really important one was a new building for the Glasgow School of Art. The school was on a restricted, steeply sloping site. Mackintosh contrived a building that was simple, functional and elegant. By the time it was completed in 1909 it was greatly admired by European architects, but it attracted little attention in Britain, and he designed only half a dozen more buildings.

In 1913 he moved to London, where he and his wife designed fabrics and furniture. In 1920 they retired to the south of France, where Mackintosh devoted himself to painting watercolours. In 1927, suffering from cancer, he returned to England for treatment, and died a year later.

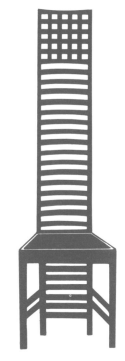

A Mackintosh chair

A perspective drawing for a school in Glasgow

Sir Edwin Lutyens

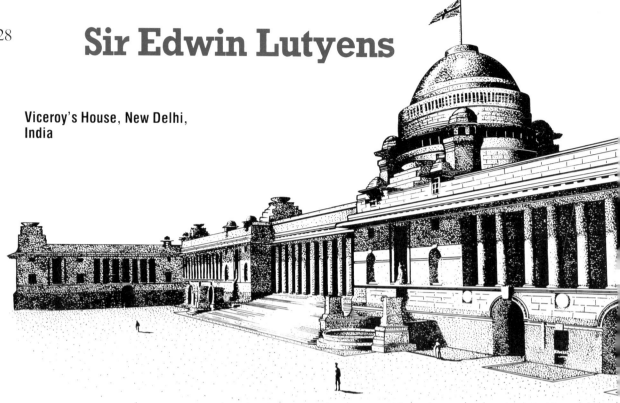

Viceroy's House, New Delhi,
India

To see Edwin Lutyens's finest building means a visit to New Delhi. His masterpiece is the Rashtrapati Bhawan, the president's palace, which Lutyens built as the Viceroy's House in the last years of British rule in India. This building, begun in 1912 and finished in 1931, is one of the largest palaces ever constructed.

Edwin Landseer Lutyens was born in 1869, the 11th child in a family of 14. Because of poor health young Edwin was educated mainly at home, and he was always shy, though he had a keen wit.

He went briefly to art school, and spent two years with a London firm of architects. In 1889 a family friend asked him to design a small country house, and on the strength of this commission Lutyens set up in business on his own

Some years later he met the landscape gardener Gertrude Jekyll, for whom he built a house, Munstead Wood in Surrey, the first of many

houses. Lutyens's skill with country houses was in making them blend with their surroundings. He used old bricks or new ones chosen for their mellow colouring.

Gertrude Jekyll had a great influence on Lutyens. She helped to form his style, designed gardens for many of his houses, and introduced him to important clients.

To make sure of obtaining commissions for important buildings Lutyens set out to master the classical styles of ancient Greece and Rome. This mastery led to his being asked to design the Viceroy's House, and also the city plan for New Delhi.

Lutyens designed the Cenotaph in Whitehall to honour the dead of World War I, university buildings at Oxford and Cambridge, and offices in London. He received a knighthood and the Order of Merit.

1869
Born 29th March in London
1896
Built Munstead Wood for Gertrude Jekyll
1904
Designed *Country Life* offices
1908-1909
Consulting architect to Hampstead Garden Suburb
1912-1931
Built the Viceroy's House in New Delhi
1917
Member of Imperial War Graves Commission
1918
Received knighthood
1919
Designed Whitehall Cenotaph
1926-1929
Designed British Embassy in Washington, DC
1944
Died 1st January in London

Jane Drew

Shops in Accra, Ghana

Jane Beverly Drew is particularly noted for her work on the architecture of tropical lands, on which she became an internationally-recognised expert. She was one of the earliest women to achieve world fame in architecture.

Jane Drew was born at Thornton Heath, Surrey, and studied architecture in London. She married her first husband, James T. Alliston, a fellow architect, while still studying. She and Alliston formed a working partnership, but it and their marriage broke up in 1939. During World War II Jane Drew had her own office and employed other women architects.

In 1942 she married another architect, Edwin Maxwell Fry. The same year she became interested in the architecture of hot climates, and began with a project in Kenya. Two years later she and Maxwell Fry were appointed advisers on town planning for Britain's then colonies in West Africa. From their experience in Africa came a book, *Village Housing in the Tropics,* which was

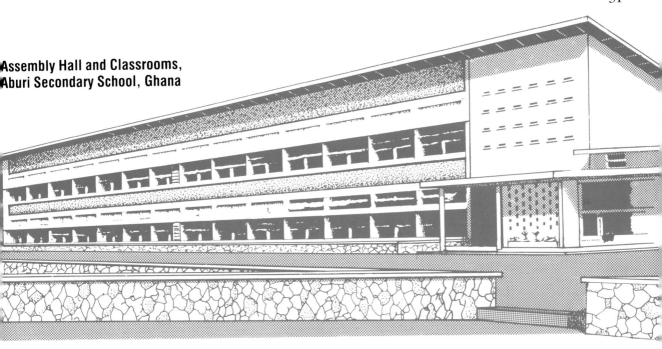

Assembly Hall and Classrooms, Aburi Secondary School, Ghana

largely Jane Drew's work, though she had two co-authors. She collaborated on two other books on tropical architecture which became standard textbooks.

In 1945 the firm of Fry, Drew and partners was formed. Jane Drew and Fry were appointed to work on the new city of Chandigarh, which the Swiss architect Le Corbusier was designing as a new capital for the Indian state of East Punjab. Jane Drew's part was in the creation of housing for 20,000 people, plus schools and buildings for community use.

Besides India and Kenya, Jane Drew designed buildings in Ghana, Iran, Kuwait, Mauritius, Nigeria and Sri Lanka. She is especially known for her work on complex buildings such as hospitals and universities. Notable examples in Britain include the Open University at Milton Keynes, and the School for the Deaf at Herne Hill in London. From 1945 to 1974 she was editor of the Architects' Year Book, which she founded.

1911
Born 24th March in Thornton Heath, Surrey
1928-1933
Studied architecture in London
1932-1939
Married to J.T. Alliston
1934-1939
In practice with Alliston
1942
Married E. Maxwell Fry; worked in Kenya
1944-1945
Designed buildings in West Africa
1951-1956
Worked in Chandigarh
1965
Built Olympic Stadium at Kaduna, Nigeria
1969-1970
First woman president of the Architectural Association
1969-1977
Built Open University

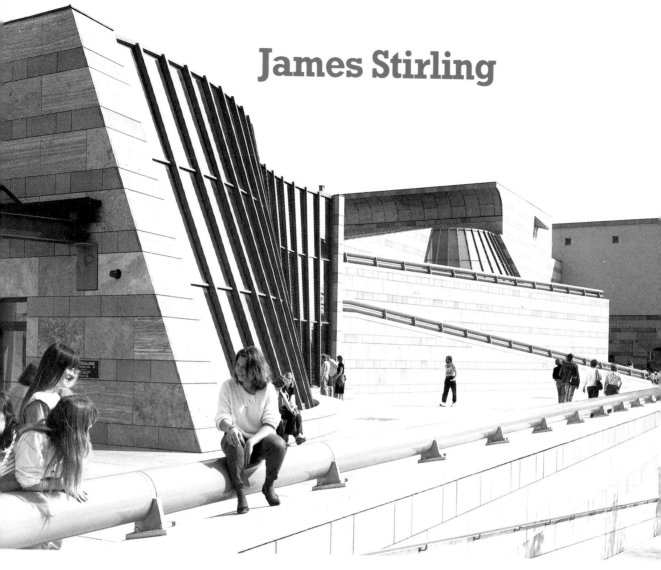

James Stirling

Stuttgart Art Gallery

James Stirling is one of the most controversial figures in modern architecture. He was born in Glasgow, and following four years' war service with the Parachute Regiment studied architecture at Liverpool University. After some years with a London firm of architects he went into partnership with James Gowan. The first large commission the partners received was for the Engineering Department at Leicester University, an award-winning 'iceberg' of a building.

For some years Stirling was in business on his own, and during that time he completed two more university buildings, one for Queen's College, Oxford, and the other for the History Faculty at

Cambridge - a futuristic-looking structure of glass and steel.

During the building of Runcorn New Town (1967-1976), a low budget housing estate midway between Liverpool and Manchester, Stirling formed a partnership with Michael Wilford. Together they designed three major building projects in Cologne, Dusseldorf and Stuttgart in Germany. One, the Staatsgalerie (State Art Gallery) in Stuttgart, has many examples of Stirling's wayward sense of humour, including a piano-shaped music department and a group of stones which have apparently fallen off the facade. They are the only genuine solid stones in the building - the rest are thin cladding.

More recently he has received a number of commissions in the United States, including museum buildings for the universities of Harvard and Columbia, and was awarded the Pritzker Prize in 1981.

1926
Born 22nd April in Glasgow
1942-1945
War service with the Parachute Regiment
1945-1950
Studied architecture at Liverpool University
1956-1963
Partner of James Gowan
1959-1963
Built Leicester University Engineering Department
1966
Married; designed Florey Building in Oxford
1967
Completed History Faculty building in Cambridge
1967-1976
Built Runcorn New Town
1971
Formed partnership with Michael Wilford
1980
Awarded RIBA Gold Medal

Housing, Runcorn New Town

Norman Foster

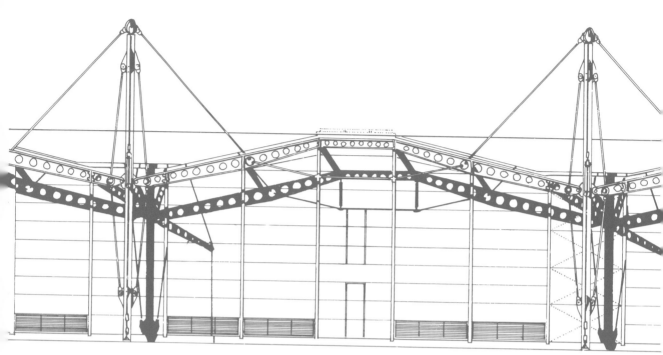

**The Renault Works
in Swindon, Wiltshire**

Norman Foster is regarded as one of the leading pioneers in using modern high technology in architecture. He does not use 'high-tech' for its own sake, but chooses the technology appropriate to each structure. He claims, 'high technology buildings are hand-crafted with the same care as bricks and mortar or timber.'

Norman Robert Foster was born in Manchester in 1935, and studied architecture at the University of Manchester and at Yale University in the United States. In 1963 he and three other young architects founded Team 4, a group operating from one room in a London flat. The other members were his future wife Wendy, her sister Georgie Wolton, and Richard Rogers. Rogers was later famous as the designer of the Pompidou Centre in Paris. The group first attracted attention with an elegant factory building for Reliance Controls at Swindon, which deliberately avoided the usual distinction between the accommodation

for 'workers' and 'management'.

Team 4 lasted for four years. When it broke up Foster founded Foster Associates, which now has nine associates and a total staff of nearly 50.

The firm's outstanding buildings include the Willis Faber Office at Ipswich, planned around a bank of escalators; the Sainsbury Centre for the Visual Arts at Norwich, a lightweight, steel and glass pavilion; a parts distribution centre for Renault cars at Swindon; and the new tower-like headquarters for the Hong Kong Bank, in which the floors are suspended from eight tubular steel masts.

Foster believes in prefabricated components, which can be tested to destruction in the factory before they are approved for use. He makes full-sized mock-ups of various parts of a building to make sure that they do what he and the client want.

Willis Faber Office, Ipswich

1935
Born 1st June in Manchester
1953-1955
Served in Royal Air Force
1956-1961
At Manchester University
1961-1962
Fellowship at Yale University
1963-1967
Partner in Team 4, London
1964
Married Wendy Cheesman
1967
Founded Foster Associates
1975
Completed Willis Faber Office
1978
Completed Sainsbury Centre for the Visual Arts
1979-1986
Built Hong Kong Bank
1986
Completed the Hammersmith Centre, London

Places of interest

The location of a selection of major buildings by the architects in this book

Inigo Jones

1 Monument to Lady Cotton, Norton-in-Hales Church, Shropshire
2 South Facade of Wilton House, near Salisbury, Wiltshire
3 Banqueting House, Whitehall, London
  Church of St Paul, Covent Garden, London
  The Queen's House, Greenwich, London

Sir Christopher Wren

1 Sheldonian Theatre, Oxford, Oxfordshire
2 The chapel of Pembroke College, Cambridge, Cambridgeshire
3 St Paul's Cathedral, London
  Royal Hospital, Chelsea, London
4 The Courthouse, Windsor, Berkshire

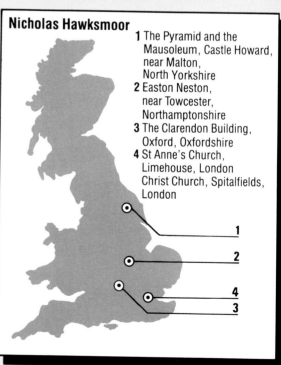

Nicholas Hawksmoor

1 The Pyramid and the Mausoleum, Castle Howard, near Malton, North Yorkshire
2 Easton Neston, near Towcester, Northamptonshire
3 The Clarendon Building, Oxford, Oxfordshire
4 St Anne's Church, Limehouse, London
  Christ Church, Spitalfields, London

Sir John Vanbrugh

1 Seaton Delaval, near Blyth, Northumberland
2 Castle Howard, near Malton, North Yorkshire
3 The Orangery, Kensington Gardens, London
4 Blenheim Palace, near Woodstock, Oxfordshire
5 King's Weston, near Bristol, Gloucestershire

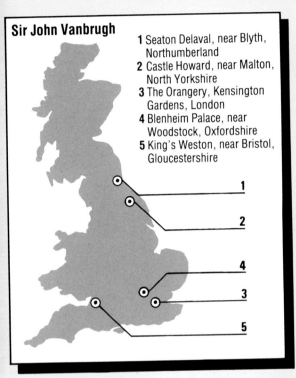

Robert Adam

1 The Register House, Edinburgh, Lothian, Scotland
2 Culzean Castle, near Maidens, Strathclyde
3 Kedleston Hall, near Derby, Derbyshire
4 Theatre and Market Hall (now Town Hall), Bury St Edmunds, Suffolk
5 Osterley Park House, Isleworth, Middlesex

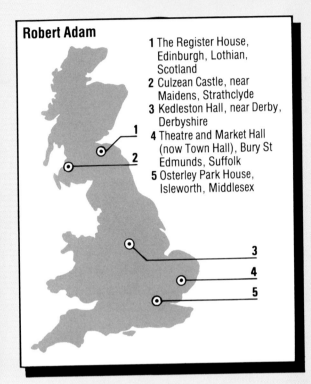

John Nash

1 House at Cronkhill, Shropshire
2 Cumberland Terrace, Regent's Park, London
3 Cottages at Blaise, near Bristol, Avon
4 Royal Pavilion, Brighton, Sussex
5 Market House and Guildhall, Newport, Isle of Wight

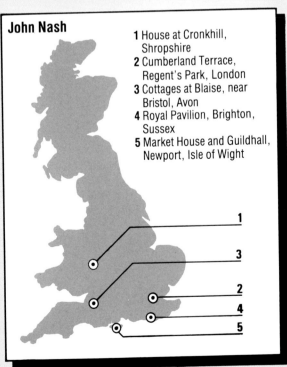

Sir John Soane

1 Pellwall House, near Market Drayton, Staffordshire
2 Wiston Hall, Wissington, Suffolk
3 Dulwich Art Gallery, Dulwich, London
No. 14, Lincoln's Inn Fields, London
4 Pitzhanger Place, Ealing, Middlesex

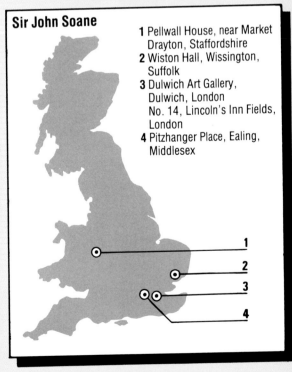

Places of interest

Sir George Gilbert Scott

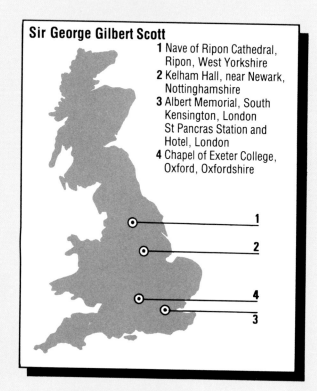

1 Nave of Ripon Cathedral, Ripon, West Yorkshire
2 Kelham Hall, near Newark, Nottinghamshire
3 Albert Memorial, South Kensington, London
  St Pancras Station and Hotel, London
4 Chapel of Exeter College, Oxford, Oxfordshire

Norman Shaw

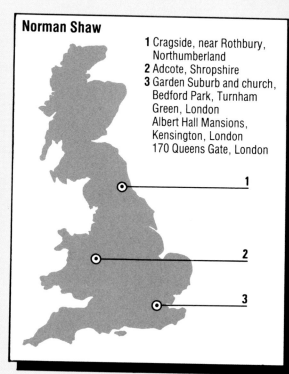

1 Cragside, near Rothbury, Northumberland
2 Adcote, Shropshire
3 Garden Suburb and church, Bedford Park, Turnham Green, London
  Albert Hall Mansions, Kensington, London
  170 Queens Gate, London

Charles Voysey

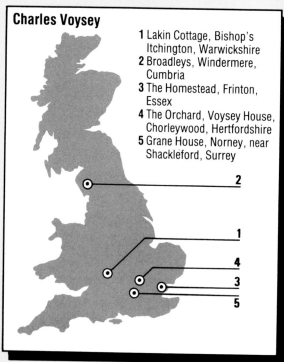

1 Lakin Cottage, Bishop's Itchington, Warwickshire
2 Broadleys, Windermere, Cumbria
3 The Homestead, Frinton, Essex
4 The Orchard, Voysey House, Chorleywood, Hertfordshire
5 Grane House, Norney, near Shackleford, Surrey

Charles Rennie Mackintosh

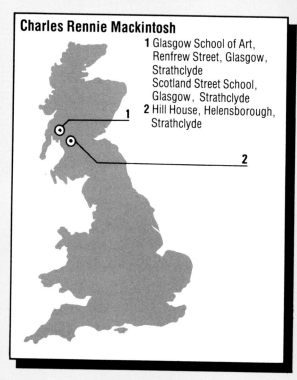

1 Glasgow School of Art, Renfrew Street, Glasgow, Strathclyde
  Scotland Street School, Glasgow, Strathclyde
2 Hill House, Helensborough, Strathclyde

Sir Edwin Lutyens

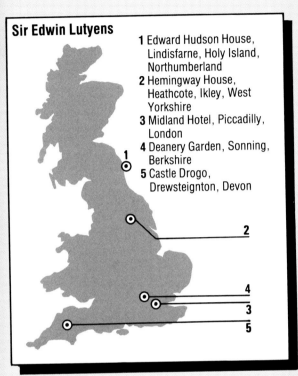

1 Edward Hudson House, Lindisfarne, Holy Island, Northumberland
2 Hemingway House, Heathcote, Ikley, West Yorkshire
3 Midland Hotel, Piccadilly, London
4 Deanery Garden, Sonning, Berkshire
5 Castle Drogo, Drewsteignton, Devon

Jane Drew

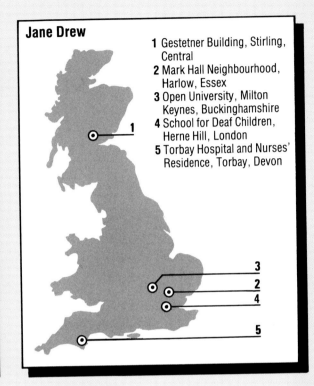

1 Gestetner Building, Stirling, Central
2 Mark Hall Neighbourhood, Harlow, Essex
3 Open University, Milton Keynes, Buckinghamshire
4 School for Deaf Children, Herne Hill, London
5 Torbay Hospital and Nurses' Residence, Torbay, Devon

James Stirling

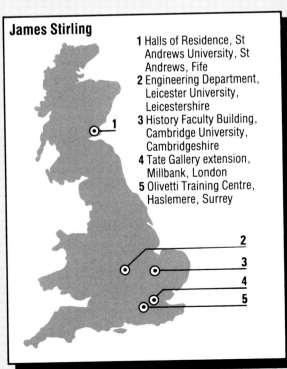

1 Halls of Residence, St Andrews University, St Andrews, Fife
2 Engineering Department, Leicester University, Leicestershire
3 History Faculty Building, Cambridge University, Cambridgeshire
4 Tate Gallery extension, Millbank, London
5 Olivetti Training Centre, Haslemere, Surrey

Norman Foster

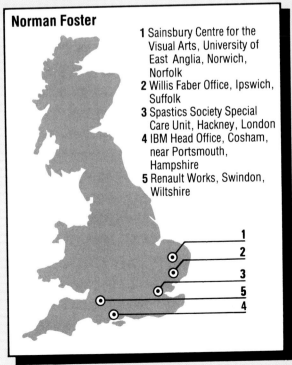

1 Sainsbury Centre for the Visual Arts, University of East Anglia, Norwich, Norfolk
2 Willis Faber Office, Ipswich, Suffolk
3 Spastics Society Special Care Unit, Hackney, London
4 IBM Head Office, Cosham, near Portsmouth, Hampshire
5 Renault Works, Swindon, Wiltshire

Useful addresses

Architectural Association,
34 Bedford Square,
London WC1

The Registrar,
Architects Registration Council of the U.K.,
73 Hallam Street,
London W1N 6EE

Building Industry Careers Service,
82 New Cavendish Street,
London W1M 8AD

Chartered Institute of Building Services,
Delta House,
Balham High Road,
London SW12 9BS

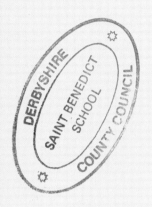

Chartered Institute of Building,
Englemere,
Kings Ride,
Ascot,
Berks, SL5 8BJ

Construction Surveyors Institute,
Wellington House,
203 Worship Lane,
East Dulwich,
London SE22 8HA

Incorporated Association of Architects and Surveyors,
Jubilee House,
Billing Brook Road,
Weston Favell,
Northampton

Royal Institute of British Architects,
66 Portland Place,
London W1N 4AD

Royal Institute of Chartered Surveyors,
18 Great George Street,
London SW1P 3AD

Index

SCIENTISTS

EXPLORERS

BACON

BOYLE

NEWTON

FROBISHER

HUDSON

COOK

HALLEY

THE
HERSCHELS

JENNER

PARK

FRANKLIN

STURT

DALTON

FARADAY

DARWIN

ROSS

LIVINGSTONE

SPEKE

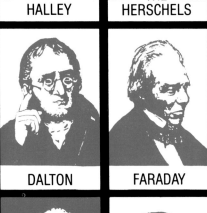

KELVIN

LISTER

MAXWELL

STANLEY

YOUNGHUSBAND

SCOTT

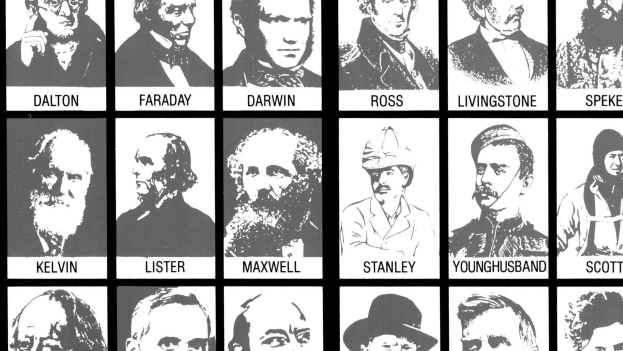

THOMSON

FLEMING

CRICK

SHACKLETON

FUCHS

FIENNES